TECH **TITANS**

# SAMSUNG

BY MICHAEL REGAN

CONTENT CONSULTANT

Pratool Bharti
Graduate Research Assistant
University of South Florida

**Essential Library**

An Imprint of Abdo Publishing | abdobooks.com

# ABDOBOOKS.COM

Published by Abdo Publishing, a division of ABDO, PO Box 398166, Minneapolis, Minnesota 55439. Copyright © 2019 by Abdo Consulting Group, Inc. International copyrights reserved in all countries. No part of this book may be reproduced in any form without written permission from the publisher. Essential Library™ is a trademark and logo of Abdo Publishing.

Printed in the United States of America, North Mankato, Minnesota.
092018
012019

**THIS BOOK CONTAINS RECYCLED MATERIALS**

Cover Photo: Manu Fernandez/AP Images
Interior Photos: John Locher/AP Images, 4–5, 7; David Becker/Getty Images News/ Getty Images, 9; Nashriq Mohd/Shutterstock Images, 13; Red Line Editorial, 15, 81, 75; Underwood Archives/Archive Photos/Getty Images, 16–17; Yonhap/AP Images, 19; Teesside Archive/Mirrorpix/Getty Images, 23; Shutterstock Images, 24, 69; Paul Popper/Popperfoto/Getty Images, 26–27; AP Images, 29; Yonhap News/YNA/ Newscom, 31, 93; Kurita KAKU/Gamma-Rapho/Getty Images, 35; Patrick Robert/ Corbis/Sygma/Getty Images, 36–37; Ahn Young-joon/AP Images, 41, 59, 67; Chung Sung-Jun/Getty Images News/Getty Images, 42–43; Martial Trezzini/AP Images, 46; Paul Sakuma/AP Images, 48; Pasieka/Science Source, 51; Justin Sullivan/Getty Images News/Getty Images, 52–53; Lee Jae Won/Reuters/Newscom, 55; Roman Arbuzov/Shutterstock Images, 62; Lee Jin-man/AP Images, 64–65; Lee Young-ho/ Sipa USA/AP Images, 71; Leszek Kobusinski/Shutterstock Images, 76–77, 85; Audrey McAvoy/AP Images, 79; Kobby Dagan/Shutterstock Images, 86–87; Jon Simon/ Feature Photo Service/Samsung/AP Images, 90; Kyodo/Newscom, 95; Victor Wong/ Shutterstock Images, 96

Editor: Arnold Ringstad        MAR 2 6 2019
Series Designer: Laura Polzin

**Library of Congress Control Number: 2018948317**

**Publisher's Cataloging-in-Publication Data**

Names: Regan, Michael, author.
Title: Samsung / by Michael Regan.
Description: Minneapolis, Minnesota : Abdo Publishing, 2019 | Series: Tech titans | Includes online resources and index.
Identifiers: ISBN 9781532116919 (lib. bdg.) | ISBN 9781532159756 (ebook)
Subjects: LCSH: Samsung Entertainment Group--Juvenile literature. | Samsung televisions--Juvenile literature. | Cell phones--Juvenile literature. | Technology --Juvenile literature.
Classification: DDC 338.762138--dc23

# CONTENTS

# CHAPTER ONE

# A WIDE-RANGING COMPANY

The South Korean company Samsung is best known to consumers for its smartphones and TVs. But those are only some of the products Samsung produces. At the Consumer Electronics Show (CES) in January 2018, the company put on view a wide range of new products and applications. TVs, software, kitchen appliances, speakers, and medical devices were all on display.

## TVs AND DISPLAYS

One of the products that gained the most attention was a TV that Samsung called "The Wall." It had a whopping 146-inch (371 cm) screen.[1] The large screen was made up of smaller modules. The number of modules can

**Virtual reality headsets were among the high-tech gadgets that Samsung showed off at the 2018 Consumer Electronics Show.**

## BIXBY AND ARTIFICIAL INTELLIGENCE

Samsung's personal assistant software, Bixby, allows its users to interact with other Samsung products, including smartphones, TVs, and kitchen appliances. Samsung is putting millions of dollars into hiring researchers to develop machines that learn what human users want and then perform those actions without being told to do so.

Artificial intelligence (AI) systems show some abilities similar to human intelligence. They include planning, reasoning, learning, problem-solving, perception, and the ability to manipulate objects. AI is divided into two types: narrow AI and general AI. Narrow AI examples are vision recognition systems for self-driving cars and the voice recognition of the Siri or Bixby virtual assistants. Narrow intelligence systems can be taught or learn how to carry out a specific task. General AI, by contrast, is true humanlike intelligence. It can learn to do many different kinds of tasks. It's the kind of AI seen in science fiction movies, and it does not exist yet in reality.

be increased or decreased to make the screen any size the customer wants. Under bright light, the edges of the modules could be seen, but when the TV was turned on, those edges disappeared. All of the company's new TVs have built-in voice control software, which Samsung calls Bixby. Introduced in 2017, it is similar to Amazon's Alexa voice service and Apple's Siri. It lets people ask for their favorite shows, learn about the weather, turn on the lights, or show photos.

Samsung's TVs have other interesting new elements. Now only one fiber-optic cable comes out the back. Power and all audio-visual signals are carried through that mostly hidden cable. Steam Link, a system that enables games from computers to be played on a big-screen TV, will be supported on all Samsung TVs. The company also introduced a new 49-inch (124 cm) computer gaming monitor that is responsive and sharp.

In an effort to help offices and maybe even classrooms go entirely paperless, Samsung presented the Flip. It's a digital whiteboard that connects easily with phones and laptops. This makes instantaneous collaboration between project partners in offices or schools possible. The large screen can be set either horizontally or vertically.

**Samsung is a major player in the large-screen TV industry.**

## CONNECTING EVERYTHING

### SMARTTHINGS CLOUD SERVICE

Samsung entered into cloud computing through its SmartThings device and service. The word *cloud* simply refers to the internet. Cloud computing is the storing and accessing of data and programs over the internet. Cloud computing is big business. In 2015, this type of computing was worth an estimated $67 billion. That figure was expected to rise to $162 billion by 2020.[3]

Samsung has long been a manufacturer of electronics hardware. The company has also begun working on its own software to go with those devices. One of Samsung's goals is to have all electronic devices connected through a single system. To do that, it developed its SmartThings cloud service. Even smart cars will be connected through SmartThings, which includes a hub device and an accompanying online service. HS Kim, one of Samsung's CEOs (chief executive officers), explained, "SmartThings will be your remote control for your connected devices."[2]

Those connected devices include not only televisions and monitors but even kitchen appliances. Samsung's refrigerators are getting smarter. The interior cameras can tell whether the ingredients for a particular recipe are already in the fridge. The smart TV on the front can play favorite programs or cooking videos. The company even upgraded the fridge's built-in speaker system.

Samsung also showed off appliances for the laundry room. Its compact QuickDrive washing machine, only 24 inches (61 cm) wide, will fit in a closet or small space. Samsung said the washer would clean the clothes faster than regular washers. It also has a small door through which forgotten items can be added during the wash cycle without getting water all over the floor.

Samsung demonstrated new speakers at the event, too. One was a sound bar designed to go with the company's wall-mounted TVs. Another was a wireless

**A CES attendee examines one of Samsung's new smart refrigerators.**

speaker only a few inches thick and two feet (61 cm) wide. Volume control is through a magnetic dial that looks like a hockey puck. It can be attached to any metal surface. The speakers are Wi-Fi connected and are controlled by the SmartThings app.

## COMPUTER CHIPS

Samsung has long been a leading computer chip manufacturer. In 2018, its most advanced chip to date was incorporated into its newest smartphone, the Galaxy S9. The chip was an award winner in the embedded technologies category at the CES 2018 show. The new chip will also be used in personal computers.

The fast and powerful chip is expected to help Samsung get further into the artificial intelligence (AI) field. The company aims to be an industry leader in AI someday. However, Samsung has some catching up to do in this area. Google Assistant and Amazon's Alexa personal assistant had advantages in technology and popularity as of early 2018.

## MEDICAL DEVICES

Samsung also featured two medical devices that were created in the company's research program, C-Lab. One of them, GoBreath, is for patients with lung damage. The portable device helps patients learn methods of breathing that will speed their recovery time after surgery. Their doctors can check on their progress remotely through the internet.

A second product, Relumino smart glasses, was also introduced. The glasses help people with vision problems see better when they are reading or just looking at objects. An accompanying phone processes videos from a camera in the glasses. Those images are then sent back to a display on the glasses, allowing the person to see the image more clearly.

## HEALTH-CARE ROBOTS

Samsung's participation in the health-care and AI fields has great potential. The combination could make health care more efficient, friendly, and accurate. However, public trust issues about machine learning and AI have to be addressed.

Who is responsible if health-care AI makes the wrong decision? What is the risk of AI health care being used to hurt people? Experts in technology and ethics are studying such questions. The Nuffield Council on Bioethics, an independent organization based in the United Kingdom, stated in one of its reports, "AI technologies have the potential to help address important health challenges."[4] But the report also indicated that AI might be limited by the quality of the data it has access to and whether it can mimic important human qualities such as compassion.

# SAMSUNG'S TRANSFORMATION

Although Samsung makes lots of money from smartphones, televisions, appliances, and computer chips, it did not start out as an electronics firm. The Korean company came into being long before the country was divided into North and South Korea in 1945. Lee Byung-chul started the company in 1938. Korea was under occupation by Japan at that time. Originally, the company milled rice and transported goods.

As time went on, the company expanded into many other fields. Sugar refining, textile manufacturing, and goods trading in the early 1950s provided the foundation of the Samsung Corporation. By the mid-1960s, Samsung was involved in fertilizers, a private university, insurance, and food processing, among other activities. It was not until 1969 that the company established Samsung Electronics as a subsidiary. In the 1970s, Samsung Electronics's first products were TVs. The company later

Samsung sells its many products at retail locations around the globe.

expanded into other household appliances. At the same time, the Samsung Corporation was still expanding into industries such as shipbuilding and heavy chemicals. Clothing manufacturing and hotels were also targets of Samsung's expansion.

Samsung grew internationally during the 1990s. Various subsidiaries were involved in large construction projects and aerospace manufacturing. Samsung has bought, sold, and affiliated with numerous companies over its life span. In 2017, there were 59 affiliated companies within the company's largest division, Samsung Group.[5] Samsung Electronics was just one of those companies, but it brought in the most money for the group. In 2012, Samsung Electronics became the largest manufacturer of mobile phones.

Samsung Electronics had humble beginnings but became an international powerhouse. There were periods when Samsung's future looked bleak. But with hard work, governmental support, and an adventurous spirit, the company flourished. By 2018, it was one of the world's most successful consumer electronics companies.

# SMARTPHONE MARKET SHARE, SAMSUNG VS. APPLE, 2009-2017[6]

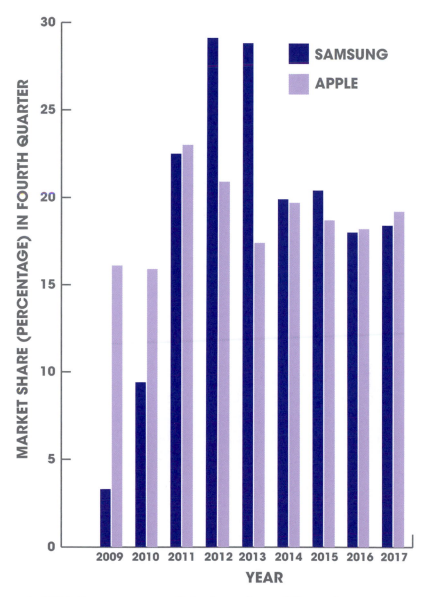

In 2012, Samsung overtook Apple as the world's number one smartphone manufacturer by market share. The two companies' fourth-quarter market share remained similar between 2014 and 2017.

# CHAPTER **TWO**

# FOUNDATIONAL YEARS

The Samsung conglomerate came into existence in 1938 as a rice mill and small transportation company in Masan, Korea. Started by Lee Byung-chul, the company originally had only 40 employees. Masan, now a district of Changwon, was the largest port city in southeastern Korea. The Japanese occupying forces used the Masan port as a drop-off point for materials going to their war efforts throughout Asia.

## JAPANESE OCCUPATION

During the war between Japan and China that started in 1937, Lee moved his company to Taegu, Korea. There he started an export business to send food and merchandise to Manchuria, a region of China. Manchuria was also under Japanese occupation. Lee also opened a flour

**Samsung got its start during the Japanese occupation of Korea.**

## KOREA UNDER OCCUPATION

The Samsung businesses benefited from both the Japanese occupation and US control. From 1910 to 1945, Korea was occupied by Japan. At first, the occupiers were harsh on the Koreans. They relented somewhat after a nationwide protest against Japanese colonialism in 1919. Although the Japanese rule was oppressive, several aspects of Korean life improved. Urbanization increased, commerce expanded, and Korea's industrialization took root. Although the purpose of this industrialization was mostly to enrich Japan, the foundation was laid for Korean businesses to take over these industries after the Japanese were defeated in 1945 and expelled from the Korean peninsula.

mill and a cotton-processing plant in Taegu. In 1943, Lee further expanded by acquiring liquor companies using family money and Japanese bank loans.

During World War II (1939–1945), when Korea was still occupied by the Japanese, Samsung rapidly became an important trucking business. Samsung did not make huge profits at that time. However, Lee learned how to manage a business well. His success during this period later resulted in criticism, with historians noting that Samsung and other powerful Korean businesses got started by collaborating with the Japanese occupiers. Because any business in Korea during the occupation needed Japanese permission to operate, there may have been some truth to that assertion.

# LEE BYUNG-CHUL

Lee Byung-chul was the founder of Samsung. Born in 1910, he died of lung cancer in 1987. He was born into a wealthy landowning family. He studied at, but did not graduate from, Waseda University in Japan. Instead, he returned home to be involved in several family businesses.

Lee was married to Park Du-eul and had four sons and six daughters. Several of those children eventually came to run various aspects of the Samsung empire. Besides having a reputation as a hard worker, Lee had a strong business sense and was intelligent. Lee was a hands-on business manager. He tightly managed the company and knew everything that was happening. He was said to have sat in on the hiring interviews of every new Samsung employee from 1957 to 1986. Like most of the other chaebol leaders in South Korea, he could also be ruthless in his business dealings.

Lee believed the most patriotic thing a business could do was create wealth that would strengthen the nation in which it was started. Based on that belief, he was always investing in or starting companies that would benefit his country. Then he built them into successful businesses that enriched not only himself but his country too.

In Samsung, Lee started a company that would continue growing and prospering long after his death.

# US MILITARY ADMINISTRATION

When Japan was defeated in World War II, Korea came under the control of the Soviet Union and the United States. These two nations, allies during the war, became bitter rivals in the decades after their victory. The Soviet Union controlled the North, and the United States oversaw the South. The two sides could not agree about a unified government, so two countries were formed: North Korea and South Korea. Samsung continued to be successful in South Korea in the years after the war. One of the reasons was that the Japanese abandoned large amounts of military supplies in Korea and Manchuria. Samsung was able to sell those supplies for huge profits. As the company grew, it moved to the larger South Korean city of Seoul in 1947.

In June 1950, with the outbreak of the Korean War (1950–1953), the company moved its headquarters to Busan. Samsung had to abandon its businesses because the North Koreans had overrun most of Korea, except Busan. Lee maintained his close relations to the South Korean government. When the Korean War ended in a stalemate in 1953, the Korean peninsula remained divided. Lee opened a sugar refinery in South Korea and then expanded into textiles and opened a wool mill.

In a few years, Lee became known as the richest man in Korea. He was also considered to be a corrupt businessman by some because of what they believed were too-cozy relationships with the South Korean government.

# THE START OF THE SAMSUNG EMPIRE

Samsung opened three businesses that marked its birth as an industrial empire. In 1951, it started the trading company Samsung Corporation. In 1953, it started Cheil Foods and Chemicals. This company was in charge of processing sugar, flour, and canned foods. Then, in 1954, Samsung launched Cheil Wool and Textile Corporation. It was a clothing business.

## THE KOREAN WAR

Between 1945 and 1950, the Russians and Chinese built up military forces in North Korea. At the same time, the United States did not help build up South Korea's military forces. By the middle of June 1949, the United States had withdrawn its occupation forces. When North Korea attacked the South in June 1950, it had almost 200,000 troops, along with tanks and planes supplied by the Soviet Union. The South Korean army had fewer than 100,000 troops, with no tanks, heavy artillery, or planes.[1] The South was easily overrun.

The United States did not want to be seen as allowing aggressive actions by the communist Soviets and Chinese. The only thing that saved the South was quick intervention by US and United Nations (UN) forces. The US and UN forces retaliated in June 1950, pushing back the invasion and quickly taking over most of North Korea. At that point, the Chinese sent in soldiers to oppose the US and UN armies. The fighting ended three years later with a truce that kept the country divided by a heavily fortified and fenced demilitarized zone (DMZ). More than three million Koreans, one million Chinese, and 54,000 Americans were killed in the fighting. Korea remained a divided country as of 2018.[2]

All three of those companies were strongly supported by the South Korean government. The government granted them monopolies in their industries. Not surprisingly, those companies found enormous success. The clothing business alone grew at a rate of more than 90 percent per year between 1956 and 1960.[3]

But it did not stop there. In 1957, Samsung bought a security company and a cement company. Between 1957 and 1959 it acquired three banks from the Korean government. In 1958, it purchased the first of its fertilizer and fire insurance companies. In the 1950s, Samsung laid the foundation for its becoming a chaebol conglomerate. A chaebol, which means "wealth clique" in Korean, is a collection of independent companies that are all under the control of a single family. A chaebol is

## CHAEBOLS

After World War II, chaebols were seen as a way to quickly grow Korea's underdeveloped economy. It worked. But as time went on, some people felt the chaebols had too much power through corruption and payoffs to high government officials. In 2017, South Korea's then president, Park Geun-hye, was sentenced to 24 years in prison for corruption involving the chaebols.[4]

Korean citizens have started to question the consolidation of wealth among a small group of families. The chaebols are also seen as stifling new businesses. According to Kim Sang-jo of Hansung University, South Koreans are no longer willing to overlook illegal and improper connections between the government and the chaebols. Government regulators and company investors are putting on pressure to limit the chaebols. In 2018, the top South Korean chaebols were Samsung, Hyundai, SK, LG, and Lotte.

Samsung's industrial efforts have long been a key part of its business empire.

**LG is one of several chaebols that control much of South Korea's economy.**

usually an enormous, complex, and powerful industrial group. By the end of the 1950s, Samsung was the largest company in South Korea.

## FRIENDS AT FIRST

Samsung was not the first electronics company in South Korea. The chaebol LG, started by Koo In-hwoi, held that honor. Like Samsung, LG had started in other business endeavors prior to entering the electronics field.

Koo named his electronics company Goldstar in 1958. It later became LG Electronics. The company is still successful today.

Lee and Koo came from the same province in South Korea. They attended the same elementary school. They were said to be good friends and mutually respected each other. They started a broadcasting company together that became successful. In 1956, they also became in-laws. Lee's second daughter, Lee Sook-hee, married Koo's third son, Koo Ja-hak. Relations between the two families went along well until Samsung decided to enter the electronics business itself in 1969.

## A FAMILY BUSINESS

As of 2015, Samsung was the seventh-largest family-owned business in the world.[5] The Lee family continues to hold the company into a third generation. Lee Kun-hee, son of Samsung founder Lee Byung-chul, has grown the business into a worldwide leader. Lee Kun-hee's son, Jay Y. Lee, as well as two of his daughters, Boo-jin and Seo-hyun, also became top executives within the company.

# CHAPTER THREE

# FAMILY AND FRIENDS

n May 1961, the South Korean military staged a coup and took over the nation's government. This could have been a major setback for Samsung because the military seemed to be cracking down on corrupt businessmen. Lee found out he was at the top of that list. At the time, Lee was in Japan in the house he owned with his Japanese wife. He decided to return to South Korea and hold meetings with Park Chung-hee, the head of the military regime. The two agreed Lee would be forgiven for his past actions as long as he used his company to help transform South Korea into a competitive industrial country.

The goal of the South Korean military government was to change the country from one of the poorest Asian nations into a worldwide industry leader. The country had little in the

Cooperation with military dictator Park Chung-hee allowed Samsung to thrive in the 1960s and 1970s.

way of resources, money, and industrial expertise. On the other hand, it had lots of cheap and organized workers. The government began importing raw materials and technology, using local factories to build products, and then exporting those products to other countries.

Park thought the only way to do this was through big family-owned companies, the chaebols. So he picked several dozen companies and gave them special privileges and government support. Samsung was one of those companies. Business experts outside the country did not think this approach to industrialization would work. It was thought the chances of corruption would be too great. Even though some corruption did happen, it was not as great as observers feared. From the 1960s on, Samsung was one of South Korea's largest and most successful companies.

## SECOND WAVE OF MAJOR EXPANSION

The Samsung Group expanded tremendously during the 1960s. It started a new fertilizer company in 1961 and then bought a fire insurance business in 1962. Samsung quickly followed up with the purchase of three more insurance firms in 1963. In that same year,

**The military coup in South Korea led to significant changes in the structure of the nation's economy.**

it bought a department store, a security firm, and a real estate business. The year 1964 saw the addition of another fertilizer company, Hankuk Fertilizer, and a private university. In 1965, Samsung established the Korea Hospital, the Samsung Cultural Foundation, a food seasoning company, and a paper manufacturing firm. The company was on an expansion binge. However, it had not yet entered the electronics field that would eventually make it a household name around the globe.

Samsung's first brush with a public scandal happened in 1966. Hankuk Fertilizer was caught smuggling 55 short tons (50 metric tons) of the sugar substitute saccharin, disguised as building materials, into the country.[1] Lee's second son, Lee Chang-hee, was sentenced to jail. Because of this scandal, Lee stepped down from actively leading the company and turned over the fertilizer company to the government of South Korea. His oldest son, Lee Maeng-hee, took over in 1967. However, this leadership change did not last long.

Lee Maeng-hee had an abrasive leadership style, and his father's closest associates disliked him. The elder Lee wrote in his memoirs, "I gave part of the group's management to my oldest. . . . And before even six months had gone by, the entire group was in chaos."[2] It was apparent that Samsung's founder did not support his son's management style.

Within two years, Lee Maeng-hee lost further favor with his father. He was rumored to be responsible for a letter sent from his jailed brother, Lee Chang-hee, to the president of South Korea claiming their father was involved in the saccharin smuggling scandal. The action to implicate Lee Byung-chul in wrongdoing led him, in

1969, to remove his two eldest sons from the succession list to become the head of the Samsung Group. He then took back the role of chair of Samsung.

**Lee Maeng-hee was at the center of a Samsung leadership struggle in the late 1960s.**

## OUTSIDE HELP

The Samsung Group, with Lee Byung-chul back in charge in 1969, started the subsidiary company Samsung Electronics to diversify into the emerging electronics industry. Samsung did not have the technology necessary to create and build electronic devices. To get the technology for these businesses, Samsung partnered with several transnational corporations (TNCs), corporations that operate in multiple countries at one time. These included the Japanese companies Sanyo and Nippon Electric Corporation.

### SAMSUNG VS. LG

In 1969, the South Korean government announced a plan to support electronics businesses. Even before the government's announcement, Samsung prepared to get into the electronics business. Lee Byung-chul told his friend Koo In-hwoi, who ran the existing electronics company Goldstar, what he was going to do. Koo yelled at Lee. Koo did not think that Lee should become a competitor to his company. Lee was shocked by the response and left the meeting. They were never friends again, and the competition between Goldstar and Samsung—which means "three stars" in Korean—began. The rivalry became known as the war of the stars. Lee was not deterred by his former friend's objections and launched Samsung into the electronics business.

Those companies gave money and technology to Samsung for a share of any profits from the sale of the resulting items. Samsung started by producing outdated black-and-white TVs in 1970. Later in the decade, it began producing other appliances, including refrigerators, microwaves, color TVs, and computer monitors. But for 20 years, the company's products were considered cheap and low quality by consumers, and they were sold mainly at discount stores.

# MORE EXPANSION

To keep prices low, Samsung started several other companies to make the parts for its appliances. Samsung Corning made the glass for picture tubes, critical parts of old-fashioned televisions. Samsung SDI manufactured the picture tubes. Samsung Electro-Mechanics made other electronic parts for the company's appliances.

Samsung did not limit itself to new businesses in electronics. In the early 1970s,

## TRANSNATIONAL CORPORATIONS

Samsung is one of the largest transnational corporations (TNCs). A TNC is a large company that does business in more than one country. A benefit of TNCs is that they can often provide products and services at lower prices than smaller local companies. However, there are disadvantages too.

TNCs often manufacture their products in countries where wages are very low. Those TNCs then take the low-wage products and sell them in other countries. The profits are taken away to other locations. A local company not only pays the wages to local employees but also keeps the profits circulating in the local economy.

Another drawback to TNCs is that they usually have to transport large quantities of products. That transportation uses fossil fuels. The resulting environmental damage pollutes the atmosphere and leads to climate change.

A third disadvantage of TNCs is that they can lead to economic instability. If a country has many small corporations, then one company failing does not affect the overall economy. However, in countries dominated by only a few TNCs, one company's failure can lead to catastrophic results for the whole country.

it moved into heavy chemical products, making things such as agricultural chemicals, paints, plastics, and fibers. Samsung's machinery business made parts for things such as ships, automobiles, spacecraft, helicopters, and trains. Later, the company expanded even further, into the areas of civil engineering, housing construction, and highway and road building. Samsung's 1970s expansions were highlighted by heavy industry and electronics. The company even opened a theme park.

## IMPORTANCE OF INFORMAL TIES

It wasn't just luck or strong business management practices that helped Lee build an empire. His children and grandchildren married other people who were powerful in Korean society. Those in-laws either joined Samsung businesses or were powerful in their own businesses. These leaders helped Samsung keep strong control of the company.

Different regions of Korea play an important role in business and government connections. Using his connections based on schooling and hometowns, Lee developed relationships with elites from Kyongsang Province. It was the most powerful region of Korea. He hired retired government and military officials and gave

**Samsung's entrance into the world of high-tech electronics would change the company forever.**

them high positions within Samsung businesses. These connections helped him obtain political favors.

Keeping the business within the family also helped Samsung remain powerful. In the traditional Korean chaebol, the business was passed down from father to son. Lee Byung-chul willed Samsung to his third son, Lee Kun-hee, who then passed it along to his son Jay Y. Lee. The women in the family were not left out. Lee Kun-hee's daughters hold high positions in two of Samsung's subsidiaries. The same was true for Lee Byung-chul's other sons and daughters.

# CHAPTER FOUR

# RISE OF THE COMPUTER

D uring the 1980s, Samsung focused its resources on electronics and research and development activities. It entered the telecommunications hardware business when it bought out another company in 1980. At first, it built telephone switchboards. Later, it started manufacturing telephones, fax systems, and mobile phones.

## SAMSUNG JOINS THE CLUB

In 1983, Lee Byung-chul announced the company's formal move into the semiconductor business. Semiconductors are materials in which the movement of an electrical current can be controlled. They make computer chips possible. Lee's new initiative was a bold move because it took billions of dollars to start up semiconductor manufacturing. It was also a very competitive

**Samsung's factories turned out circuit boards in the 1980s, moving the company deeper into the high-tech economy.**

## MAKING COMPONENTS

Samsung still makes many parts of its devices itself, including its smartphones. This allows the company to quickly increase the production of those parts for new additions to its phone line or to meet increasing demand. That ability makes Samsung phone components a favorite of other smartphone companies. In fact, one of Samsung's biggest component buyers is Apple.

"All of their competitors must use third parties to accomplish the same tasks," said Len Jelinek, a semiconductor analyst for a research firm. This is a big advantage for Samsung over its competitors. "One could estimate that there would be at least [a quarter year's] advantage due to internal control of all operations," according to Jelinek.[1]

and cutthroat industry. Several Japanese companies, including NEC, Toshiba, and Hitachi, were far and away the leading producers of computer memory chips. US companies such as Motorola, Texas Instruments, and National Semiconductor were also strong in that field.

Samsung was a latecomer to the fast-paced personal computer industry. But it quickly became competitive in the memory chips field. By the end of 1983, Samsung had produced a 64-kilobyte memory chip. By 1988, it produced its first 4-megabyte chip—more than 60 times the capacity of its 1983 chip—only six months later than its Japanese competitors. Samsung became a notable supplier of memory chips for computer and electronics manufacturers throughout the world by the late 1980s. According to Lee Sin-doo, professor of electrical engineering at Seoul National University, "It was arguably the most important decision made by Lee and Samsung . . . semiconductors would become its cash-cow."[2]

The money made from semiconductors made it possible to grow Samsung's businesses in TVs and mobile devices. Those divisions of Samsung Electronics used the money to aggressively expand manufacturing into other countries. The company opened a TV and microwave oven manufacturing facility in New York in 1984 and another in England in 1987. Between 1977 and 1987, Samsung Group's yearly sales increased from $1.3 billion to $24 billion. Its yearly revenue in 1987 made up about 20 percent of South Korea's total annual value of goods and services produced.[3]

## VIRTUAL REALITY THEME PARK

Everland theme park was a venture started by Samsung in 1976. During the 1990s and 2000s, it was ranked as one of the best theme parks in the world. In 2016, the theme park opened a virtual reality (VR) version of its Universe Big Wheel. The original Ferris wheel there had closed in 2010 after 28 years of operation. It had been one of the park's most popular rides. An Everland official said, "We believe that this will emerge as a must-take-ride, attracting large numbers of visitors."[4]

To meet customers' changing demands, the park has increased its VR attractions. The park installed VR on one of its popular family train rides. Another new addition, Gyro VR, is an outer space fighter-pilot ride where the pilots battle alien enemies. In another ride, Robot VR, the riders guide a giant robot over and around various obstacles.

# SAMSUNG FOUNDER DIES

In 1987, Samsung lost its founder when Lee Byung-chul died. His third son, Lee Kun-hee, took over as chair. Lee Kun-hee realized the importance of the electronics industry and made it a central focus. One of his first moves was to streamline Samsung's businesses.

In 1988, he merged Samsung Semiconductor into Samsung Electronics. He also reorganized Samsung so that engineering, construction, and most high-tech products were contained within the Samsung Group. That was the year Samsung introduced its first mobile phone. CJ became Samsung's holding company for food, biotechnology, and audiovisual media. Lee gathered department stores and retail into Shinsegae. Textiles were organized under Saehan. Hansol became the holder of the paper manufacturing company. Finally, JoongAng Ilbo held the convenience stores and media enterprises. Each company was run by close family members or trusted allies.

## EXPANDING CHEMICAL BUSINESS

The year 1989 marked the beginning of a partnership between Samsung and British Petroleum (BP), called Samsung BP. The new company manufactured acetic acid for sale to chemical industries. The acid is used for the manufacture of dyes, perfumes, inks, soft drink bottles, and wood glues, among other things. Acetic acid is also sold to the public in its diluted form, vinegar.

# LEE KUN-HEE

Lee Kun-hee was the chair of Samsung Group in 2018. He was the third son of Samsung's founder, Lee Byung-chul. Lee Kun-hee joined the family business in 1968. He quietly learned about the management of the company from his father. In 1987, after his father's death, he was named Samsung's chair. He left most of the operations of the company to Samsung's corporate staff. But in 1993, he launched a project called the New Management Initiative that would change the way Samsung operated. Lee initiated the changes because he felt Samsung products were considered second-rate by consumers and other businesses. His reforms made Samsung competitive with major international companies.

Lee Kun-hee is married and has three children. He suffered a heart attack in 2014, from which he had not recovered as of June 2018. His son Jay Y. Lee has run the business since then. In 2018, Lee Kun-hee was reported to be worth nearly $18 billion, making him the richest person in South Korea.[5] Hong Ra-hee, Lee's wife, is also a billionaire, due to her stock ownership in Samsung Group.

Lee Kun-hee oversaw significant growth for Samsung in the 1980s and 1990s.

# CHAPTER **FIVE**

# CHANGE IN CORPORATE CULTURE

I n the early 1990s, Samsung was stagnating. Even though the company was selling a lot of products, it didn't inspire much excitement among consumers, and profits were falling. Chair Lee Kun-hee thought this stagnation was the result of company executives doing things the way they had always been done and not getting new ideas from outside the company. He decided to shake things up.

## LEARNING NEW WAYS

In 1993, Lee Kun-hee introduced what he called the New Management Initiative. He gave workers permission to work more on their own ideas. Rather than paying the highest salaries to workers and managers who had been in the company the longest, he boosted the pay

**As times changed, Samsung searched for new ways to keep its products successful and relevant.**

of those who created the best ideas and projects. He ended the practice of giving lifelong jobs to employees. Samsung employees now had to produce actively rather than only show up for work each day. He also committed the company to greatly increasing its research and development capabilities.

Lee knew he couldn't just tell his workers to come up with new ideas for products and management styles and expect them to do that. The employees would need training on how to go about generating these new ideas. So, to prepare for the New Management Initiative, he started an externship program three years before the management initiative was announced. He sent up-and-coming younger employees to other countries to learn about their cultures and ways of thinking. This was done so Samsung's staff could learn more about products and industry developments around the globe. Those employees were called regional specialists. Since 1990, more than 4,700 Samsung employees have taken part in this program, traveling to 80 countries.[1]

Many of Samsung's managers did not like the idea of sending their top young people on a yearlong business trip out of the country. Those managers complained about the cost, and they feared their best people would be hired away from Samsung during their externship. "They simply didn't understand the purpose," said Kwon-taek Chung, a director at the Samsung Economic Research Institute.[2]

Despite the grumbling, Lee Kun-hee kept an iron grip on the company and pushed forward with the program. From the early 1990s to the present time, Samsung sent out its brightest young stars during good economic times and bad. According to Sea Jin Chang, a professor at the University of Singapore, Lee's decision to start the program was "pivotal in transforming Samsung into a global powerhouse."[3]

## PHONES ON FIRE

By the 1990s, Samsung still did not have the technology

### REGIONAL SPECIALIST PROGRAM

Samsung's yearlong regional specialist training program had several components. The first was learning the language of the country to which the specialists would be going. It included social and physical practice, too. Jogging, meditation, table manners, and dancing were parts of the program.

Specialists have gone to places such as Thailand, Indonesia, China, the United States, and Europe. Participation required some sacrifice, too, as employees were sent alone and not allowed to bring family members. On the other hand, the early spirit of the program was to socialize and have fun while learning about the country's culture. At first, only a report on social activities and contacts were required of the participants. Later, the regional specialists were also required to add business-related information to the reports.

to produce the higher-quality, and more profitable, large-sized TVs that were becoming more popular in the marketplace. The company invested in improving its TV technology and product quality. Part of Samsung's new focus on quality products and research and development came as the result of an incident in 1995. Lee Kun-hee

**Samsung sought to improve the quality of its products, including its mobile phones, in the late 1990s.**

sent out the newest Samsung mobile phones as New Year's presents. Word came back to him that the phones didn't work. He was mortified and angry.

Lee Kun-hee made a visit to the mobile phone factory at Gumi, South Korea. There he had all the phones that were in the factory placed in a big pile. He then had them set on fire. Besides getting rid of defective phones, the fire signaled to all the employees the chair's commitment to doing quality work. After the New Year's embarrassment, Samsung increased its research and development budget and started turning out higher-quality products, including phones that could play music and had high-resolution cameras.

## UP, DOWN, UP AGAIN

Samsung Electronics continued to invest heavily in making chips in the early and mid-1990s. This investment enabled Samsung to overtake its foreign competitors. It became the leading producer of memory chips in 1993. In 1994, it introduced a new and larger memory chip. Profits for the company increased by more than $1.2 billion in only one year. By the end of 1995, Samsung Electronics was exporting more than $10 billion worth of chips.[4]

In 1996, an oversupply of memory chips caused a steep decrease in price. Samsung's revenue from its formerly high-performing product dropped. To bolster its incoming revenue, the company started increasing efficiency and changing the main focus of the company away from memory chips. From 1995 to the end of 1999, chips dropped from 90 percent of company sales down to 20 percent.[5] The new focus was on telecommunications, microprocessors, and other non-memory products. Two of those items, cell phones and flat-screen TVs, became Samsung's next top products.

**Samsung tried to get an early lead in the market for flat-screen computer monitors and TVs.**

# ASIAN MONETARY PROBLEMS

The Asian financial crisis of 1997–1998 forced Samsung to sell off some of its businesses. The company cut 26 percent of its Korean workers and 33 percent of its international workers.[6] The crisis drove many companies based in Asia out of business. But Samsung made it through the hard economic times.

Analysts note that the crisis allowed the company to refocus on its main businesses. Not only that but the survival and prosperity of Samsung demonstrated the wisdom of the move to higher-quality products instead of simple mass production. Despite the

## ASIAN FINANCIAL CRISIS

In July 1997, Thailand devalued its currency in relation to the US dollar, making it worth relatively less, to strengthen the country's faltering economy. Devaluing a currency can be a good thing by increasing exports, decreasing trade deficits, and reducing total payments on government debt. However, a big drawback is that it might cause regional or worldwide recession. Thailand's move sparked a deep financial crisis in eastern Asia. Malaysia, the Philippines, and Indonesia quickly developed similar financial, and in some cases, political disasters. Cash stopped flowing into many eastern Asian countries, and their economies slowed as a result. Some of them went into a deep recession. Japanese banks stopped lending money that was necessary for businesses to survive. South Korea was on the verge of going bankrupt.

International banking organizations stepped in to loan money to the affected countries to help them stabilize their economies. The strong international support and internal financial reforms by the affected countries eventually stopped the crisis and laid the foundation for a strong recovery.

trying financial times, Samsung generated significant gains in sales during this period.

# CONSUMER ELECTRONICS

One of Samsung Electronics's goals was to beat the Japanese companies, such as Sony, that had led the electronics industry worldwide. To do that, Samsung needed to succeed in the consumer electronics field. The company invested heavily in developing digital flat screens. In 1998, Samsung Electronics gained the top spot for liquid crystal display (LCD) flat-panel TV screens.

On the cellular phone front, the company had invested heavily in phone design and technology. By 1995, it had become the best-selling brand in South Korea. The Asian financial crisis of 1997 spurred the push for nationwide wireless networks by the South Korean government. The government saw this as a new economic growth generator for the country and its electronics chaebols. In 1999, Samsung Electronics produced its first internet-connected smartphone. The support from the government helped Samsung Electronics gain an edge over non-Korean phone developers. This advantage paid off handsomely for Samsung in the 2000s.

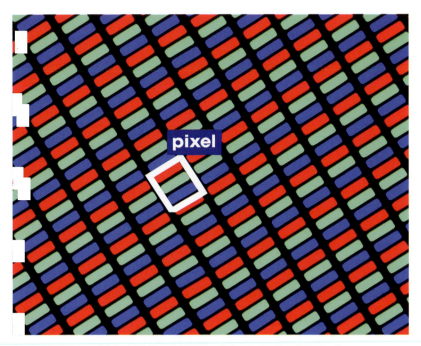

An LCD uses a thin panel made up of thousands of tiny picture elements called pixels. Each pixel is made up of three subpixels—one red, one green, and one blue. Subpixels can be lit up individually by an electric charge.

After weathering the financial crisis, Samsung Electronics was improving substantially in international competition with other electronics companies. All of its products were profitable. It had a big share of the cellular phone market and a lead in worldwide production of computer screens, and it was in the top six manufacturers of wireless home phones. The company overall had a profit of $2.4 billion, and its stock price had risen sharply.[7]

# CHAPTER **SIX**

# BECOMING AN INDUSTRY LEADER

U p until 2002, Japan's Sony was seen as the world's top electronics company. But in that year, Samsung overtook Sony in total value. Decades after the company's founding, Samsung had become one of the most profitable companies in the electronics industry.

## HOW SAMSUNG BEAT SONY

Kevin Lane Keller is a professor of marketing at Dartmouth College in Hanover, New Hampshire. Keller, an international leader in the study of brands, worked as a consultant to Samsung. According to Keller, Samsung's emergence started in 1993 with its New Management Initiative. Up to that time, Samsung was known as a high-volume, low-quality manufacturer.

**Samsung's booth at the 2003 Consumer Electronics Show showed off the tech titan's latest products.**

In a 2013 interview with *Forbes* magazine, Keller shared the reasons Samsung was able to beat Sony. Through the New Management Initiative, Samsung was able to convince its employees to focus on three things. The first was the quality of the products. Because the company itself made many of the parts that went into Samsung's products, it had enormous control over improving the quality. A second focus was improving the design of the products. Samsung opened design centers around the world and hired the best designers possible. The last thing Samsung did was to match or beat Sony's prices for similar products. According to Keller, Samsung was the first electronics company since Apple to put those three qualities together. However, he warned that Samsung must not get complacent. It needed to keep focused on those three qualities or risk losing its edge over other companies.

## LEE WOMEN IN CONTROL

Samsung is well known for keeping business affairs within the family. Lee Kun-hee's two daughters were long subject to speculation as to how they would fit into the Samsung Group. As expected, both became key parts of the company's empire.

**Lee Boo-jin made successful moves in Samsung's retail businesses.**

Lee Boo-jin turned out to be an astute businesswoman. Lee made bold moves after joining the firm. She made massive investments in duty-free stores through Hotel Shilla, a luxury hotel company that runs these stores. Travelers can buy goods at duty-free shops and not have to pay the local import taxes that are charged if purchases are made at other stores. Duty-free shops are often found at international airports, border stations, and cruise ship ports. She chose to expand overseas while closing the company's bakery

## FAST FASHION

Samsung's fashion wing under Lee Kun-hee's youngest daughter, Lee Seo-hyun, was not successful. However, similar fast fashion companies, such as Spain's Zara, H&M of Sweden, and Fashion Nova of the United States, achieved popularity. Fast fashion products are made swiftly and cheaply to get them to market as quickly as possible. This makes trendy clothing available to mainstream customers at affordable prices.

Besides being unsuccessful, those products did not seem to fit with Samsung's Eco-management goals that were introduced in 2009, which emphasize care for the environment. Fast fashion has been criticized as encouraging swiftly discarding clothing to move on to the next fashion. On an environmental level, the process contributes to pollution, low wages, poor workmanship, and harsh working conditions in developing countries where the clothes are manufactured. Some designers think their designs have been illegally copied and mass produced.

and café businesses in South Korea. Hotel Shilla's revenue went from 430 billion won ($398 million) in 2001 to more than three trillion won ($2.78 billion) in 2016.[1]

Lee Seo-hyun did not fare as well in her business ventures with the fashion arm of Samsung Construction & Trading (C&T). Her business strategy focusing on fast fashion, which involves quickly copying other designers' styles, was not a success. However, she financially supported several successful Korean designers in New York who helped raise Korean fashion to a new level. The sisters' positions of ownership within the Samsung subsidiaries made them the richest women in Korea.

# MEETING CRISES

In 2008, Lee Kun-hee was found guilty of evading taxes and was fined about $90 million.[2] He was also sentenced to a three-year prison term that would start after five years. Lee resigned as the leader of Samsung Electronics and apologized for his wrongdoing. The company also lost several other of its top leaders to retirement.

At about the same time, a global financial crisis was unfolding. Businesses, banks, and countries were in danger of going bankrupt. Fewer companies were buying memory chips, hurting one of the company's major profit centers. But just when Samsung needed strong and experienced leaders to deal with the worldwide financial crisis, they were gone.

The immediate response to the leadership crisis was to reorganize the company with younger leaders who were willing to take more creative approaches to business. The reorganization also moved the company's product focus away from its past reliance on devices such as memory chips and LCDs. The new direction focused on digital media and telecommunications. The new focus included products such as light-emitting diode (LED) TVs, smartphones, and digital appliances. Despite the worldwide financial crisis, Samsung remained profitable.

# PATH OUT OF CHAOS

In June 2009, Korea's supreme court cleared Lee Kun-hee of the criminal charges from the previous year. Lee returned to his leadership role in Samsung. His company, Samsung Electronics, turned 40 years old in November 2009. On the company's birthday, Lee Kun-hee laid out his vision for the company's continuing growth by 2020. He wanted Samsung to create products and technologies that enhanced people's quality of life worldwide. He outlined several steps the company would take to reach this lofty goal.

**The trial of Lee Kun-hee, *center*, was the subject of intense media attention in South Korea.**

Lee wanted Samsung to continue its lead in memory chips, TVs, mobile phones, appliances, computers, and printers. Along with that, the company would expand into the new fields of medical devices, health services, and solar cell manufacturing. Lee pictured Samsung welcoming collaboration with outside organizations in addition to strengthening existing relationships. He wanted the company to extend its responsibility to society in general and to develop environmentally friendly business practices.

Lee's vision would lead the company into competition with companies such as General Electric, Siemens, and

## SAMSUNG FIGHTS CLIMATE CHANGE

In 2009, Lee Kun-hee presented his year 2020 vision for Samsung. One of his main goals was to serve society by developing environmentally friendly business practices. In recent years the company has focused on reducing its effect on climate change. Even though the company added new facilities that produce more greenhouse gases, it introduced emission reduction projects that reduced the average amount of greenhouse gases produced per product. Samsung also requires renewable energy targets be met for its buildings and for such things as street lighting, transportation, and cafeterias at its plants.

Samsung joined with the graduate school of environmental studies at Seoul National University in 2015 to conduct research on adapting to climate change. One project that came from the research was a collaboration with the organization Scientists and Engineers without Borders. Using Samsung products, they installed drinking water facilities in ten Vietnamese schools that were exposed to climate change risks. Another project had Samsung engage in housing renovation projects in its home country. In 2016, the renovated homes used 57 percent less energy than they had used previous to the renovations.[5]

Philips, who were already leaders in fields such as medical technology. His vision would also lead to environmentally friendly products that would support the world's growing awareness and actions on climate change. In his 2010 book *Samsung Electronics*, businessman Tony Michell wrote, "For Samsung to succeed, it will need to focus more than ever on finding that Korean magic that helped transform the company from an industry newbie into the powerful pacesetter for the global electronics industry."[4] As the company got over a series of internal and worldwide crises, Samsung seemed to have recovered that magic.

# SAMSUNG VS. APPLE

That magic was applied to Samsung's newest mobile phones. After the Asian financial crisis a few years earlier, the government of South Korea decided to push wireless networks as a new growth industry. By 2006, South Korea had some of the fastest wireless phone networks in the world. The government support of faster networks let Korean phone manufacturers, including Samsung, get valuable experience and a lead on companies in other countries.

Apple produced its first smartphone in 2007. The iPhone's sleek design, huge touch screen, and advanced software stunned the cell phone industry. Samsung had been in the mobile phone business for more than 20 years, and it was the largest mobile phone seller in Korea. Still, it and other industry leaders had to adapt to the new smartphone era. It was not until Samsung introduced its first Galaxy S phone in 2010 that it tried to compete with Apple. Samsung's phone featured a larger, sharper screen and a high-quality camera. Those qualities were the foundation for Samsung's challenge to Apple's standing as the best-selling smartphone manufacturer.

Samsung's smartphones are known for their sharp,
high-quality displays.

# EXPANSION INTO MEDICAL DEVICES

Acting on Lee Kun-hee's goals for 2020, Samsung Electronics made a big step into the health-care field. Samsung indicated it would invest 1.2 trillion won ($1.1 billion) in this industry in May 2010.[6] In December 2010, it bought a majority share of the Korean ultrasonic medical equipment company Medison.

The resulting company, named Samsung Medison, was a new move for Samsung. Its creation again put Samsung in direct competition with established industry giants such as General Electric, Philips, Siemens, and Toshiba.

# CHAPTER SEVEN

# BUILDING ON SUCCESS

P rior to 2010, not many people in the United States associated Samsung with mobile phones. Unlike Apple, which sold phones directly to individuals, Samsung largely let cell phone companies advertise and sell its products. This changed around 2010, three years after the first iPhone was produced. The president of Samsung's mobile operations in the United States, Dale Sohn, led a team to figure out how to take control of marketing its phones. They no longer wanted to depend on outside partners to tell the Samsung phone story.

In 2011, Samsung hired Todd Pendleton, a marketing expert who had worked at the sports shoe producer Nike. Samsung had recently released its latest Galaxy smartphone, the S II. It had an innovative feature that would mute incoming calls when it was placed facedown.

**A new marketing campaign was credited with improving the sales of Samsung's Galaxy line of products.**

According to Pendleton, "We had a product that was better that was already in the market, but nobody knew about it."[1] The marketing team Pendleton put together succeeded in making consumers aware of Samsung's products. The company's ads poked fun at its competitors while showing off the unique features of Samsung's devices. By 2012, Samsung had surpassed the sales of previous phone titans Apple and Nokia.

## SMARTPHONE COMPETITION CONTINUED

Every year since 2010, Samsung and Apple have introduced new phones, Samsung in the spring and Apple in the fall. New models brought better screens, larger memory capacities, improved cameras, and other features. The two companies have continually battled in the high-end smartphone industry for several years.

Samsung and Apple battled in the courtroom, too. In 2011, Apple sued Samsung for patent infringement in the US court system. The lawsuit was over the design of smartphones, with Apple complaining that Samsung had copied the iPhone's rectangular front face with rounded edges and the arrangement of its icons on a screen. Apple won the suit. It was initially awarded almost $1 billion,

**Apple felt Samsung's Galaxy,** *left,* **infringed upon the design of the iPhone,** *right.*

but this award was reduced to $399 million.[2] In June 2018, the companies finally settled the lawsuit, with Samsung paying Apple an undisclosed amount.

At the end of 2017, smartphone sales were well over 1.5 billion units. Samsung came out on top with 20.9 percent of the sales. Next was Apple. Three Chinese device makers, Huawei, Oppo, and Vivo, rounded out the top five smartphone sellers in 2017.[3] However, during some months in 2017, China's Huawei brand outsold

Apple. Together, the three Chinese phones increased their total market share to 23.6 percent and were the fastest-growing smartphone brands.[4]

# GAMING

Samsung wants to cash in on the booming video gaming industry. Mobile phone games have revolutionized the industry. Every one of the millions of Samsung smartphones in consumers' hands around the world is a potential platform for these games. In mid-2017, global revenue for the gaming industry passed $100 billion.[5]

In gaming, Samsung is focused on hardware to make its mark. In late 2017, Samsung partnered with Microsoft to provide its QLED ultra high-definition TVs for Microsoft's Xbox One X gaming console. The Samsung monitors provide a sharp, vivid picture to bring out the best in the games' graphics. Samsung is also capitalizing on recent increases in smartphone gaming. As hardware improves, more companies are making games for mobile devices and attracting more customers. In India alone, the number of gamers was expected to grow from 120 million in 2016 to 310 million in 2021.[6]

Samsung's Gear VR headset represents a major move into the world of gaming.

Virtual reality (VR) gaming is exploding too. In 2016, industry analysts predicted that the sales of VR gaming hardware, software, and accessories would grow to $12.3 billion in 2018. Samsung's Gear VR was a part of that prediction.[7] With Gear VR, a Samsung smartphone is placed into a sensor-packed headset. The phone's screen, located right in front of users' eyes, serves as the VR display. Special lenses in the headset help create the illusion that users are seeing a virtual world around

## MEDICAL EXPANSION

Samsung Electronics continued its expansion into medical devices when it bought Nexus, a US-based health-care equipment firm. It also bought the portable medical imaging company NeuroLogica in 2013. Tod Pike, the senior vice president at Samsung's Enterprise Division, said, "The acquisition of NeuroLogica is another important step in the expansion of Samsung's medical imaging business."[8]

But in 2014, Samsung Electronics gave up on its medical ultrasound business, turning over control of the business to the Samsung Medison subsidiary. Even though the medical company was the largest ultrasound system supplier in Korea, it had only 3.1 percent of the global market. In 2013, it had made only a small $719,000 profit.[9] It was thought that this new subsidiary of Samsung Electronics would combine with Nexus and NeuroLogica, but that did not happen. Through the middle of 2016, Samsung Medison was still losing money. However, by the end of 2017, the company was turning profitable. Its sales grew 16 percent over the previous year.[10]

them. Some VR systems require dedicated headset hardware and powerful computers, making them expensive. Gear VR uses a phone that many people already own, making it a relatively affordable way for people to experience VR.

# LEGAL WOES

Jay Y. Lee is the vice chair of Samsung. He took charge of the company in 2014 because of the illness of his father, Lee Kun-hee. Jay Y. Lee was convicted in 2017 of bribing a government official. He was also convicted of embezzling company funds and hiding them overseas, as well as for lying under oath. The conviction confirmed the link between the powerful company and the South

# JAY Y. LEE

Jay Y. Lee, the vice chair of Samsung Electronics, is a native of South Korea. Also known as Lee Jae-yong in Korea, he is the grandson of Samsung founder Lee Byung-chul. He began leading Samsung Electronics following the incapacitation of his father, Lee Kun-hee. Lee earned a bachelor's degree in arts/science and a master's degree in business administration from Korean universities. He also attended Harvard Business School in the United States. He is divorced and has two children.

In April 2018, Lee was said to be worth over $8 billion by *Forbes* magazine. That made him the 207th richest billionaire in the world and the third richest in Korea.[11] In 2016, Forbes also named him the fortieth most powerful person in the world. That ranking is based upon his financial resources, his power in areas other than his business, and whether Lee uses his power to influence people and events.

**Jay Y. Lee has been recognized as one of the most powerful people in international business.**

Korean government. Lee was accused of paying bribes of $38 million to a close friend of South Korea's president, Park Geun-hye. The bribes were paid to make sure the government approved the merger of Samsung C&T and Cheil Industries. The political scandal resulted in the impeachment of President Park Geun-hye.[12]

Lee was released from prison in early 2018 after serving only one year of the original five-year sentence. That five-year sentence had been reduced, and he planned to appeal further to have all the convictions overturned. Upon being released, Lee apologized for "not showing my best side." He further said, "The past year has been a really valuable time of looking back on myself."[13]

Just days after Jay Y. Lee's release, his father was named a suspect in an 8.2 billion won ($7.5 million) tax evasion case.[14] The police were not able to question the elder Lee because he was still in a coma from an earlier heart attack. Now, he was being accused of using workers' accounts to hide money from taxation. This was not his first legal trouble relating to taxes. His 2009 conviction for tax evasion had been set aside when he became ill.

Attempts to change the structure of the Samsung Group came from both insiders and outsiders. In June

2015, the activist investor Paul Singer of Elliott Management Group in the United States bought enough shares to become the third-largest shareholder of Samsung C&T. Cheil Industries, another subsidiary controlled by the Lee family, offered to buy Samsung C&T in a move that would increase Jay Y. Lee's authority over the Samsung Group. This was the merger for which Jay Y. Lee was eventually convicted of bribing the government. The Elliott Group contended that the merger offer undervalued Samsung C&T and would be unfair to investors and only benefit the Lee family. So, Singer filed an injunction to stop the move. In July 2015, a Korean court denied the injunction.

## INHERITANCE BATTLE

In 2012, Lee Kun-hee's oldest brother, Lee Maeng-hee, and other relatives brought a multibillion-dollar inheritance civil suit against the chair of Samsung Electronics, Lee Kun-hee. They said he had hidden shares in Samsung Electronics and Samsung Life Insurance in other people's names. A lower Korean court ruled against that claim in 2013.

However, Lee Maeng-hee appealed the decision to Korea's high court. He appealed to be awarded a 700 billion won ($623 million) share of his inherited wealth.[15] In February 2014, Seoul's High Court upheld the original dismissal, saying the ten-year period for inheritance claims had passed. Lee Maeng-hee decided not to take the claim to Korea's supreme court, with his lawyers saying he "decided to give up filing for appeals as it is more important for him to keep relations with his family than to continue with the suit."[16]

Even in the face of these challenges, Samsung maintained its dominant position in the industry. It was ranked first in semiconductor revenue in 2017. It bumped US chip maker Intel from the top spot it had held since 1992. Increasing costs of computer chips due to a supply shortage led to an increase in their prices, driving up the costs of everything from computers to smartphones to automobiles. This helped drive up Samsung's profits. Despite all the family and legal turmoil for Samsung's leaders, it maintained its position as one of the largest and most successful conglomerates in the world. Samsung continued to make record profits in 2017.

**Samsung's computer chip products include solid state drives used for data storage.**

# CHAPTER EIGHT

# SURVIVING A CRISIS

S amsung Electronics was doing extremely well in the summer of 2016. Its newest smartphone, the Galaxy Note 7, was highly rated before its August release that year. *Time* magazine awarded the phone a 4.5-star rating out of a possible 5 stars.

Samsung's lines of smartphones were the biggest sellers worldwide in early 2016. They were outdueling their largest competitors, including the Apple iPhone. Then, Samsung's phone division faced its greatest crisis yet. Its smartphones' batteries started exploding.

## HISTORY OF THE DISASTER

On September 9, 2016, Jonathan Strobel was in a Costco store in Palm Beach, Florida, when his Samsung Galaxy Note 7 exploded. He said he suffered severe burns. According to Strobel, the

**The Galaxy Note 7 was at the center of one of the greatest crises in Samsung's history.**

phone burned through his pants, causing burns on his leg. He said his left thumb was also severely burned while trying to remove the phone from his pants pocket. On September 16, 2016, he filed the first exploding phone lawsuit in the United States against Samsung. This was the day after the United States Consumer Product Safety Commission officially published Samsung's recall of approximately one million of the phones that were sold in the United States. "Unfortunately for my client the recall came too late," said Strobel's attorney.[1] Strobel sought damages in the suit for more than $15,000 for "severe burns" and for leaving him in "shock and extreme pain."[2]

Strobel was not alone. Reports of the phones catching fire or exploding were reported within days of the phones' first deliveries on August 19, 2016. On August 24, a Chinese customer reported an exploding Note 7. By September 1, 2016, Samsung said there had been 35 worldwide incidents of phone fires.[3]

Samsung was reported to be preparing a worldwide recall on September 1, only a few weeks after the phones first went on sale. The following day, US mobile phone sellers AT&T, Sprint, Verizon, and T-Mobile halted sales of Galaxy Note 7s until replacements became available from

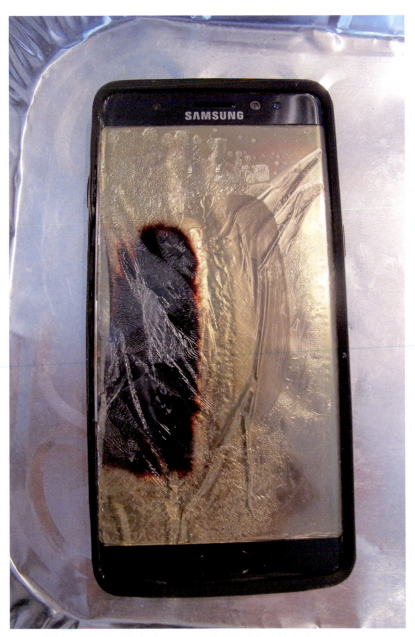

Images and stories of burned phones spread across the internet, and it soon became clear there was a widespread problem.

Samsung. The company tried to minimize the problem by saying that most of the phones would be unaffected and that "less than 0.1 percent of the entire volume sold" had problematic batteries.[4]

Samsung's problems escalated. On September 8, the US Federal Aviation Administration (FAA) advised airline passengers to turn off their Galaxy Note 7s and not attempt to charge them while on airliners. They also warned against packing the phones in suitcases.

The US Consumer Product Safety Commission ordered a recall of the Galaxy Note 7 phones on September 15, 2016. Canada and countries in Europe and Asia did the same. Samsung's earlier recall was a voluntary action by the company. The government recalls were orders to return the phones. They served as a reminder to Samsung phone users who had ignored

## HOW MANY EXPLODED?

On September 15, 2016, the US Consumer Product Safety Commission (CPSC) formally recalled the Samsung Galaxy Note 7. From the phone's release in August 2016, reports of the devices catching fire started emerging. The CPSC said Samsung had "received 92 reports of the batteries overheating in the United States, including 26 reports of burns and 55 reports of property damage, including fires in cars and a garage."[5] Worldwide, 112 of the smartphones were reported to have caught fire within a month of their release date.[6] How many phone fires went unreported is unknown.

# LARGEST PHONE RECALLS[8]

| | |
|---|---|
| SAMSUNG GALAXY NOTE 7 | REASON: FIRE RISK FROM DEFECTIVE BATTERY |
| CRICKET EZ | REASON: SOFTWARE PROBLEM INTERFERES WITH 911 CALLS |
| SAMSUNG JITTERBUG | REASON: MAY FAIL TO CONNECT TO 911 SERVICE |
| KYOCERA 7135 | REASON: FIRE RISK FROM DEFECTIVE BATTERY |
| LG 830 SPYDER | REASON: MAY FAIL TO CONNECT TO 911 SERVICE |

0    200K    400K    600K    800K    1 MIL

NUMBER OF PHONES RECALLED

**The Galaxy Note 7 recall in the United States was the largest ever for a smartphone.**

previous recall efforts. Of the nearly one million phone buyers in the United States, only 130,000 had participated in the earlier announced exchange program.[7]

# REPLACEMENTS BLOW UP TOO

On September 21, Brian Green got his replacement Note 7. Samsung had issued a software update that displayed a green battery icon on the phone's screen if it had a safe battery. Green's phone was showing this icon. Green then went on an airplane flight. As requested by the flight attendants, he turned the phone off. After putting it in his pocket, it started smoking. The plane was evacuated safely after he dropped the phone on the floor.

As stories spread of the replacement phones catching fire too, Samsung stopped exchanging the originally recalled Note 7 on October 9, 2016. Mobile phone carriers in the United States stopped exchanging or selling new Galaxy Note 7 phones. Finally, on October 11, 2016, Samsung announced it would stop selling the Note 7. A few days later, the FAA banned the phones completely from US flights. The emergency order said passengers caught bringing their phones on board could face a fine and that hiding them in luggage would result in legal charges being filed.

In the year prior to the phone battery problem, Samsung Electronics had been doing well financially. In early October 2016, the company reported third-quarter profits would be even better than the same quarter the year before. Within days of that optimistic announcement, as concerns about the problem widened, Samsung released another report adjusting its estimates. They now said the company's profit would drop 33 percent from the previous year's profit. That figure added up to a $2.3 billion loss.[9] Initially, analysts estimated that Samsung would lose $17 billion in phone sales. The company's stock declined 6.3 percent.[10] The future did not look good for Samsung.

# HOW SAMSUNG SURVIVED

The battery problem completely surprised Samsung. After its initial sluggishness in responding, the company shifted into high gear. To ensure that Note 7 owners did not try to continue using the defective phones, Samsung developed software that made the phones unusable. It also arranged messages that would be sent automatically from the phone companies, such as AT&T and Verizon, to the affected devices. The message urged Note 7 users to return the phone and get an upgrade. When the FAA banned the phones from airplanes, Samsung set up exchange stations at airports. It spent millions of dollars in determining what happened to the batteries and fixed

## WHY NOTE 7 BATTERIES FAILED

The original batteries in the Galaxy Note 7 had a manufacturing defect in one corner of the battery. There was a design flaw in an area where two parts of the battery were not supposed to contact each other. The parts were able to bend and come perilously close to each other. When they touch, the result is high heat, fire, and possible explosion. This is called a short circuit or shorting out. Some Samsung factories then stuffed the batteries in cases that were too small, thus crimping the batteries and letting the two parts touch.

Samsung had a backup for those batteries from a different supplier. They started using the second supplier for the replacement Note 7s. The replacement batteries had problems too, due to a welding error that caused them to short out. Additionally, the second batteries lacked enough insulation tape to protect their sensitive parts.

the problem. Later editions of the Galaxy phones had improved battery designs.

Other factors helped Samsung recover its footing. One was that the company's biggest rivals, Apple and Google, were not able to overtake Samsung's market share in the wake of the problem. According to the International Data Corporation (IDC), a provider of electronics market information, Samsung remained the top smartphone seller for all of 2016 and 2017.

Another reason Samsung continued to flourish was because it had additional products to rely on, including other smartphones. Samsung's Note made up only a small proportion of the company's total sales. Samsung also made other extremely popular products, such as televisions, microwaves, dishwashers, and computer memory chips. Its biggest profits come from selling smartphones and microchips, of which Samsung is the largest maker. These are used not only for its own phones but are also sold to Apple for use in the iPhone.

Carolina Milanesi of Creative Strategies, a market research firm, said Samsung also helped itself by moving on quickly to its next product rather than pausing too long to reassess its product line. A survey by market

**Samsung manufactures the screen used in the iPhone X, introduced in 2017.**

research company YouGov indicated customers have short memories. In October 2017, less than a year after its troubles, Samsung had a reputation score tied with Apple's. The YouTube videos of burning phones and the negative stories did not seem to affect Galaxy smartphone users. After the scandal, Samsung users remained loyal to their Samsung brand. Samsung's new Galaxy S8 was a hit with phone users, and the public seemed to have forgotten the problems with the Galaxy Note 7. By February 2018, Samsung had reclaimed 99 percent of the Note 7s sold in the United States.[11]

# LOOKING TO THE FUTURE

I n December 2017, Sohn Young-kwon, the president of Samsung Electronics's Strategy and Innovation Center, confirmed that future acquisitions by the company would focus on diversifying into new technology fields. Auto parts, business software, and the use of computer technology to help prevent and treat disease would be areas for future investment. Samsung would also work to acquire companies doing business in the fields of automation and data transmission.

## PROJECTED PROFIT

In order to finance future projects, Samsung would need a continuing supply of cash. That appeared to be happening, according to Samsung Electronics's reported estimates of

**Samsung hopes to maintain its dominance in technology not just by advancing its consumer electronics but also by entering a variety of other high-tech industries.**

operating profit in early 2018. The company's estimated profit had jumped a record-high 56 percent.[1]

The company was making less money on cell phone display screens because of reduced orders from Apple for its iPhone X. But record demand for Samsung's memory chips, used by a variety of smartphone makers and electronics manufacturers, buoyed the bottom line. Helping profitability were strong sales of Samsung's own new smartphone, the Galaxy S9.

# INTERNET OF THINGS

The idea behind the Internet of Things (IoT) is that any device can be connected to other devices via the internet. For example, a smartphone can connect to a coffee maker, a refrigerator, or a fitness tracker. It is estimated that six billion IoT capable devices will be in homes by 2021.[2]

Samsung Electronics sees IoT as another potential moneymaker in the form of smart homes. A smart home is one in which a smartphone, tablet, or computer can control such things as a home's lighting, temperature, cameras, locks, appliances, or entertainment system. The company prepared to make all of its products ready to connect to the IoT by 2020. Samsung's SmartThings app, which debuted in the spring of 2018, allows users to control any of these devices from their smartphone. Smart home connections to a user's car through the internet is next on the list. Automaker BMW began a partnership with SmartThings in early 2018. From inside the car, a driver could start preheating the oven for dinner or turn on a robotic vacuum cleaner. The car could also alert the driver to water or gas leaks in the home using IoT sensors. As IoT devices began to spread throughout people's homes, the possibilities seemed endless. Samsung planned to be at the forefront of developing them.

## FUTURE HOMES

Samsung envisions a future in which people can talk to their houses. Tiny microphones the size of a fingernail would be installed in lights, TVs, air-conditioning, entertainment centers, and refrigerators. All would be controlled by voice commands that go through Bixby, Samsung's voice assistant, with no need to type instructions into a smartphone or computer. Samsung's setup enables users to make voice commands in any room without speaking loudly. This appears to be an advantage over Amazon Echo and Google Home, which are located in a single spot in a house. Proponents point to the convenience of such systems, such as parents being able to check the camera in the baby's room while watching TV. On the other hand, critics wonder whether people really want everything they do at home stored in a cloud server that could potentially be hacked.

IoT has the potential to make life easier and quicker for many people. A teen's wake-up signal on her alarm clock could contact the toaster in the kitchen to start

**Samsung views the IoT as a critical part of the future of technology.**

toasting a breakfast pastry. While eating breakfast, she could use her smartphone to start her pickup truck out in the cold, snowy driveway so it's warm when she jumps in. Once on the road, the pickup could connect with the local weather station to learn whether any roads are blocked by snow, and then it could notify her school office that she might be a little late as she finds an alternate route. The school office could connect with the same weather station to verify that the student isn't trying to skip school with a fake excuse. Devices that connect to the IoT can make scenarios like this possible.

# AUTO SECTOR

In its search to find the next big thing to boost its profit margins, Samsung is looking at the automotive field. Samsung Electronics's chief strategy officer, Young Sohn, thinks the automobile sector will be similar to the smartphone experience for the company. Sohn said the company is "very excited about . . . the potential" to bring convenience and technology to the driving experience.[3] The company is looking forward to the spread of self-driving car technology. Its experience with computer chips and smart devices has given Samsung crucial background knowledge for getting into this area.

Samsung has already made inroads into the automotive field. In March 2017, the company bought a large US car audio company, Harman, for $8 billion.[4] It also set up funds to invest in auto start-up companies. Further, Samsung has established a business unit for self-driving cars.

## AI AND THE IoT

Samsung Electronics embarked upon increasing the connectivity of all its devices through the IoT. An integral part of this is machine learning and AI. In early 2018, Samsung made known that every device it manufactures will not only be IoT capable but also AI capable by the year 2020. On January 16 and 17, 2018, it demonstrated its dedication to AI by sponsoring a special event that featured world academic and industrial AI experts in Mountain View, California.

In 2017, Samsung said it was not going to start manufacturing its own cars. But it did get permission from South Korea to test self-driving vehicles that use Samsung software and sensors. The company obtained similar permission in California. The Korean permit indicated the company was going to test self-driving systems designed to handle bad weather. Like other components Samsung has created, the system could be sold to companies that plan to make self-driving cars.

In early 2018, Samsung SDI, a division that focuses on batteries and energy technology, leaped into the electric vehicle (EV) battery market in a big way. SDI used research and development funds from the 2015 sale of Samsung's chemical business. The company's new battery material can power a vehicle for more than 370 miles (600 km) on only a 20-minute charge.[5] This is farther and faster than most batteries currently used in EVs.

## THE FUTURE OF EDUCATION

Samsung is also involved in the future of learning technology. In a partnership with the University of South Australia, the company opened the new Samsung SMARTSchool in South Australia in early 2018. The aim of the high-technology school is to help teachers and students prepare for the future. According to the 2016 United Nations Sustainable Development Goals report, challenges related to cost and accessibility prevent 124 million children worldwide from receiving a good education.[6]

Samsung is using its electronics and telecommunications expertise to help governments and organizations provide classrooms for underserved students throughout the world. The classrooms include individual computer tablets and software. An interactive

**Samsung opened a school in rural Brazil in 2012.**

electronic whiteboard can display either internet-based information or student work. According to Samsung, students and teachers can share screens, teachers can monitor students' screens remotely, students can work together in small groups, and teachers can administer quizzes and polls.

# THE FUTURE OF TV

Just as it did in 2006, Samsung wants to get ahead of its TV competitors. Back then, Samsung succeeded by pushing the latest television technology. In that case, the technology was flat-panel LCD screens. That move helped set the company up as the leader in TV sales. However, the competition for high-end TV technology today is fierce. At the 2018 CES, Samsung unveiled enormous TVs based on MicroLED. This screen technology uses smaller LEDs than traditional televisions. The company is betting that MicroLED will replace the current industry-standard screens, which use LCDs and organic LEDs (OLEDs).

Because both MicroLEDs and OLEDs produce their own light, they don't need backlight like older LCD screens. They both have better contrast controls because they can produce a deeper black color. Also, both use less power than LCDs, thus saving consumers money on their electric bills while being friendlier to the environment. The advantage of MicroLEDs is that they will last longer and can be made in bigger or smaller screen sizes than OLEDs.

Although MicroLED technology has been known for a while, no one until now has attempted to manufacture the screens for mass consumption because they are more difficult to produce. Despite that, Samsung announced

**Samsung's bet on MicroLED screens is one of many high-stakes chances it has taken on emerging technology throughout its history.**

Samsung's willingness to take chances on high-tech innovations has helped propel it into the lead in many high-tech industries.

plans to push forward with the technology. By taking a risk with MicroLEDs before anyone else, Samsung hopes to create a market for them and capture the largest market share.

Samsung is not a company that has ever shied away from its competitors or hesitated with new ideas. Historically, it successfully expanded into fields in which it did not have experience or expertise. Samsung's business model of expansion, its continued focus on quality products, its willingness to spend billions of dollars in start-up costs, and its ability to overcome challenges have kept it at the forefront of the electronics industry. Throughout the company's 80-year history, it has had numerous eras of feast or famine. Despite setbacks, the company's founder and successors tenaciously kept the company going and expanding. Their business expertise and fortuitous timing, along with outside governmental support, helped make Samsung the tech titan that it is today.

# TIMELINE

## 1938

Lee Byung-chul starts Samsung, a rice mill and transportation company, in Taegu, South Korea.

## 1945

Korea comes under US administration after Japan is defeated in World War II; Samsung becomes successful selling abandoned Japanese military supplies.

## 1950–1953

The Korean War, fought between the US-backed south and the Soviet-backed north, is fought and ends in a stalemate.

## 1957–1959

Samsung continues to expand into the fields of security, cement, finance, and insurance.

## 1961–1965

Samsung continues to expand by acquiring more fertilizer, fire insurance, retail, and real estate companies.

## 1966

Lee Byung-chul steps down as Samsung chair when one of his fertilizer companies is caught smuggling saccharin into the country.

## 1969

Lee Byung-chul returns to the role of chair of Samsung; the Samsung Group starts Samsung Electronics to get into the electronics business.

## 1970s

Samsung starts producing black-and-white TVs; later it begins producing appliances such as refrigerators, microwaves, color TVs, and computer monitors.

## 1983
Samsung Electronics spends billions to enter the semiconductor business; it also starts making memory chips.

## 1987
Lee Byung-chul dies; his third son, Lee Kun-hee, takes over as the chair of Samsung.

## 1993
The New Management Initiative is introduced to enliven the stagnant company.

## 1997–1998
The Asian financial crisis forces Samsung to sell off some subsidiaries and lay off workers around the world.

## 1998
Samsung Electronics becomes the top seller of LCD flat-panel TV screens.

## 1999
Samsung produces its first smartphone.

## 2002
Samsung eclipses Sony as the most valuable electronics company in the world.

## 2010
Samsung becomes an early competitor for the Apple iPhone when it introduces its first Galaxy S phone; Samsung also expands into the medical equipment field with the purchase of an ultrasound company.

## 2012
Samsung Electronics's Galaxy smartphones take over the number one spot in worldwide smartphone sales.

## 2017
Samsung's semiconductor revenue moves it into the top spot worldwide among chip makers.

# ESSENTIAL **FACTS**

## KEY PLAYERS

### FOUNDER

- Lee Byung-chul

### LEADERSHIP

- Lee Byung-chul

- Lee Kun-hee

- Jay Y. Lee

## KEY STATISTICS

- By the end of the 1950s, Samsung became the largest company in Korea.

- Samsung became the leading manufacturer of semiconductor memory chips throughout the world in 1993.

- In 2012, Samsung smartphones took over as the best-selling phones in the world.

- In 2015, Samsung was the seventh-largest family-owned business in the world.

## IMPACT ON HISTORY

Lee Byung-chul founded the Samsung Corporation in 1938 in Korea. His businesses alternately struggled and prospered under occupation by the Japanese, under administrative rule by the United States, and during the Korean War. The company launched its amazing growth in the early 1950s, when the Korean government granted monopolies to three of Samsung's companies. By the end of the 1950s, Samsung was the largest company in South Korea, making up a significant portion of the nation's economy. In the 1960s and 1970s, the company entered the electronics industry. Today, its TVs, smartphones, and appliances are known to consumers around the world. Samsung remains one of the largest family-run organizations in the world.

## QUOTE

"It was the most important decision made by Lee and Samsung . . . semiconductors would become its cash-cow."

*—Lee Sin-doo, professor of electrical engineering at Seoul National University, 2015*

# GLOSSARY

**abrasive**
Irritating or harsh; having an annoying or grating effect on others.

**acquisition**
The purchase of one company by another.

**activist investor**
A person who purchases a stake in a company for the purposes of creating a change within that company.

**affiliate**
To officially connect to an organization.

**artificial**
Produced by humans rather than occurring naturally.

**chaebol**
A large Korean business conglomerate usually owned by a single family.

**consultant**
A person who offers expert advice professionally.

**coup**
A sudden illegal seizure of control of a government.

**devalue**
To reduce the value of something, like money.

**diversify**
To enlarge or vary a company's range of products or field of operations.

## incapacitation

A deprival of strength, power, or consciousness.

## industrialization

The development of industry on a wide scale within a country or region.

## initiative

An act or strategy intended to resolve a difficulty or improve a situation.

## injunction

A legal order that stops a person from starting or continuing an action that threatens another's legal rights.

## monopoly

Exclusive control over a commodity or service.

## occupation

The control of an area by a foreign military.

## subsidiary

A company that is owned and largely controlled by another company.

## tax evasion

The avoidance of paying taxes that are legally owed.

# ADDITIONAL **RESOURCES**

## SELECTED BIBLIOGRAPHY

Kim, Chunhyo. *Samsung, Media Empire and Family: A Power Web.* Routledge, Taylor & Francis Group, 2016.

Michell, Tony. *Samsung Electronics and the Struggle for Leadership of the Electronics Industry.* Wiley, 2010.

Tudor, Daniel. *Korea: The Impossible Country.* Tuttle, 2012.

## FURTHER READINGS

Cummings, Judy Dodge. *Apple.* Abdo, 2019.

Foran, Racquel. *South Korea.* Abdo, 2013.

Naber, Therese. *How the Computer Changed History.* Abdo, 2016.

## ONLINE RESOURCES

**Booklinks**
**NONFICTION NETWORK**
**FREE!** ONLINE NONFICTION RESOURCES

To learn more about Samsung, visit **abdobooklinks.com**. These links are routinely monitored and updated to provide the most current information available.

## MORE INFORMATION

For more information on this subject, contact or visit the following organizations:

**CONSUMER ELECTRONICS SHOW**

ces.tech/About-CES.aspx

The show, usually held in Las Vegas, Nevada, displays products from electronics manufacturers and from developers and suppliers of electronic hardware and software. Thousands of companies exhibit their technologies at the show.

**LIVING COMPUTERS: MUSEUM + LABS**

2245 First Ave. S.

Seattle, WA 98134

206-342-2020

livingcomputers.org

The museum houses computers from the 1960s to the present. In addition, it has hands-on exhibits on virtual reality, robotics, self-driving cars, and computer-generated music and art.

# SOURCE **NOTES**

## CHAPTER 1. A WIDE-RANGING COMPANY

1. Shara Tibkin. "Samsung at CES 2018: Everything the Tech Giant Announced." *CNET*, 8 Jan. 2018, cnet.com. Accessed 2 May 2018.

2. Alfred Ng. "Samsung's SmartThings Cloud Is Coming This Spring." *CNET*, 8 Jan. 2018, cnet.com. Accessed 2 May 2018.

3. Louis Columbus. "Roundup of Cloud Computing Forecasts, 2017." *Forbes*, 29 Apr. 2017, forbes.com. Accessed 21 Aug. 2018.

4. James Holloway. "Tough Questions Posed for the Use of AI in Healthcare." *New Atlas*, newatlas.com. Accessed 21 Aug. 2018.

5. Jung Suk-yee. "Samsung Group as Conglomerate Disbanded and 'New Samsung' on Test Now." *Business Korea*, businesskorea.co.kr, 2 Mar. 2017. Accessed 3 May 2018.

6. "Global Market Share Held by Leading Smartphone Vendors from 4th Quarter 2009 to 2nd Quarter 2018." *Statista*, 2018, statista.com. Accessed 21 Aug. 2018.

## CHAPTER 2. FOUNDATIONAL YEARS

1. Andrea Matles Savada and William Shaw, eds. "South Korea: A Country Study." *CountryStudies*, 1990, countrystudies.us. Accessed 17 May 2018.

2. "Korea as a Colony of Japan, 1910–1945." *Asia for Educators*, 2009, afe.easia. columbia.edu. Accessed 21 Aug. 2018.

3. Chunhyo Kim. *Samsung, Media Empire and Family: A Power Web*. Routledge Taylor & Francis Group, 2016. 32.

4. Peter Pae. "South Korea's Chaebol." *Bloomberg*, 6 Apr. 2018, bloomberg.com. Accessed 18 Apr. 2018.

5. Corey Stern. "The 21 Biggest Family-Owned Businesses in the World." *Business Insider*, 15 July 2015, businessinsider.com. Accessed 2 Apr. 2018.

## CHAPTER 3. FAMILY AND FRIENDS

1. Chunhyo Kim. *Samsung, Media Empire and Family: A Power Web*. Routledge Taylor & Francis Group, 2016. 33.

2. Kim Jin-cheol. "Samsung Squabble Speaks to History of Discord." *Hankyoreh*, 25 Apr. 2012, English.hani.co.kr. Accessed 8 Apr. 2018.

## CHAPTER 4. RISE OF THE COMPUTER

1. Michal Lev-Ram. "Samsung's Road to Global Domination." *Fortune*, 22 Jan. 2013, fortune.com. Accessed 16 Apr. 2018.

2. Cho Mu-Hyun. "The Chaebols: Samsung and LG's 50-Year 'Star Wars.'" *CNET*, 9 Apr. 2015, cnet.com. Accessed 8 Apr. 2018.

3. "Samsung Electronics Co., Ltd." *Reference for Business*, n.d., referenceforbusiness.com. Accessed 8 May 2018.

4. Lee Hyo-sik. "Everland Korea Turning into IT Theme Park." *South China Morning Post*, 25 Nov. 2016, scmp.com. Accessed 12 May 2018.

5. "Lee Kun-hee." *Forbes*, n.d., forbes.com. Accessed 6 Apr. 2018.

## CHAPTER 5. CHANGE IN CORPORATE CULTURE

1. Verne Harnish and *Fortune* Eds. *The Greatest Business Decisions of All Time. Fortune* Books, 2012. 48–49.

2. Harnish and *Fortune* Eds, *The Greatest Business Decisions*, 49–50.

3. Harnish and *Fortune* Eds, *The Greatest Business Decisions*, 49–50.

4. "Samsung Electronics Co., Ltd." *Reference for Business*, n.d., referenceforbusiness.com. Accessed 8 May 2018.

5. "Samsung Electronics Co., Ltd."

6. "Samsung Electronics Co., Ltd. History." *Funding Universe*, n.d., fundinguniverse.com. Accessed 21 Aug. 2018.

7. "Samsung Electronics Co., Ltd."

## CHAPTER 6. BECOMING AN INDUSTRY LEADER

1. Cho Chung-un. "Behind High Life, Samsung Heiress on Tough Road to Top." *Investor*, 20 July 2016, theinvestor.co.kr. Accessed 15 May 2018.

2. Lucinda Shen. "Meet Samsung's Billionaire Lee Family, South Korea's Most Powerful Dynasty." *Business Insider*, 19 June 2015, businessinsider.com. Accessed 7 Apr. 2018.

3. Song Jung-a. "Crisis Hits Profits at Samsung Electronics." *Financial Times*, 23 Oct. 2008, ft.com. Accessed 21 Aug. 2018.

4. Tony Michell. *Samsung Electronics and the Struggle for Leadership of the Electronics Industry*. John Wiley & Sons, 2010. 235.

5. "Samsung Electronics Sustainability Report 2017." *Samsung*, 2017, samsung.com. Accessed 9 June 2018.

6. "Samsung Buys Medison in Major Push to Healthcare." *Reuters*, 13 Dec. 2010, reuters.com. Accessed 13 May 2018.

## CHAPTER 7. BUILDING ON SUCCESS

1. Micahal Lev-Ram. "Samsung's Road to Global Domination." *Fortune*, 22 Jan. 2013, fortune.com. Accessed 16 Apr. 2018.

2. Joe Rossignol. "Apple vs. Samsung Lawsuit to Drag into Eighth Year with Retrial Scheduled Next May." *Mac Rumors*, 26 Oct. 2017, macrumors.com. Accessed 13 May 2018.

3. "Top 5 Best-Selling Smartphone Brands in the World." *Businesstech*, 23 Feb. 2018, businesstech.co.za. Accessed 12 May 2018.

# SOURCE NOTES

4. "Top 5 Best-Selling Smartphone Brands in the World."

5. Nate Lanxon. "China Just Became the Games Industry Capital of the World." *Bloomberg*, 31 May 2017, bloomberg.com. Accessed 15 May 2018.

6. Rahul Sachitanand. "Gaming Industry Is Seeing a Boom as Firms Cash In on Everything." *India Times*, 12 Feb. 2018, economictimes.indiatimes.com. Accessed 15 May 2018.

7. John Gaudiosi. "Virtual Reality Video Game Industry to Generate $5.1 Billion in 2016." *Fortune*, 5 Jan. 2016, fortune.com. Accessed 17 May 2018.

8. "Samsung Electronics Gives Up on Medical Instrument Business." *BusinessKorea*, 3 Dec. 2014, businesskorea.co.kr. Accessed 14 May 2018.

9. "Samsung Electronics Gives Up on Medical Instrument Business."

10. Do Yeong Nam. "Samsung Medison in Profit after Three Years." *Digital Times*, 6 Apr. 2018, eng.dt.co.kr. Accessed 14 May 2018.

11. "Jay Y. Lee." *Forbes*, n.d., forbes.com. Accessed 4 Apr. 2018.

12. Grace Chung and Aaron Tilley. "Shocking Arrest Warrant Issued for Billionaire Samsung Head Jay Y. Lee." *Forbes*, 16 Feb. 2017, forbes.com. Accessed 10 June 2018.

13. Margi Murphy. "Samsung Heir Released from Prison Following Bribery Scandal." *Telegraph*, 5 Feb. 2018, telegraph.co.uk. Accessed 3 Apr. 2018.

14. Murphy, "Samsung Heir Released from Prison Following Bribery Scandal."

15. "Samsung Boss Sued by Brother over Father's Inheritance." *BBC*, 14 Feb. 2012, bbc.com. Accessed 14 May 2018.

16. "Samsung Chief's Brother Not to Appeal for Inheritance." *Korea Herald*, 26 Feb. 2014, koreaherald.com. Accessed 14 May 2018.

17. Seo Young-ji. "Truth about Samsung's Union-Busting Management Approach May Finally Come to Light." *Hankyoreh*, 3 Apr. 2018, English.hani.co.kr. Accessed 21 Aug. 2018.

## CHAPTER 8. SURVIVING A CRISIS

1. Jonathan Stempel. "Florida Man Sues Samsung, Says Galaxy Note 7 Exploded." *Reuters*, 16 Sept. 2016, reuters.com. Accessed 23 Apr. 2018.

2. Paul Blake and Ben Stein. "Florida Man Sues Samsung after Note 7 Explodes in His Pocket." *ABC News*, 18 Sept. 2016, abcnews.go.com. Accessed 23 Apr. 2018.

3. Aditya Madanpalle. "The Samsung Galaxy Note 7 Fiasco: A Blow by Blow Account." *First Post*, 30 Dec. 2016, firstpost.com. Accessed 23 Apr. 2018.

4. Sam Byford. "Samsung Recalls Galaxy Note 7 Worldwide Due to Exploding Battery Fears." *Verge*, 2 Sept. 2016, theverge.com. Accessed 24 Apr. 2018.

5. Elyse Betters. "Official US Recall of Note 7 Fully Reveals How Many Have Exploded." *Pocket Lint*, 16 Sept. 2016, pocket-lint.com. Accessed 22 Apr. 2018.

6. Stacy Liberatore. "Samsung's Battery Woes Continue as Lawsuits Spread to Galaxy Note 5, S6, and S7 Models." *Daily Mail*, 25 May 2017, dailymail.co.uk. Accessed 22 Apr. 2018.

7. Nick Statt. "Samsung Formally Recalls the Note 7 in the US." *Verge*, 15 Sept. 2016, theverge.com. Accessed 24 Apr. 2018.

8. Aditya Madanpalle. "Samsung Galaxy Note 7 Recall: Here's a Look at a Few Device Recalls from the Past." *First Post*, 16 Sept. 2016, firstpost.com. Accessed 21 Aug. 2018.

9. Sam Byford. "Samsung Slashes Profit Forecast by a Third Following Galaxy Note 7 Debacle." *Verge*, 12 Oct. 2016, theverge.com. Accessed 25 Apr. 2018.

10. Se Young Lee. "Samsung Shares Fall after the Galaxy Note 7 Is Recalled." *Time*, 12 Sept. 2016, time.com. Accessed 17 May 2018.

11. Hayley Tsukayama. "How Samsung Moved Beyond Its Exploding Phones." *Washington Post*, 23 Feb. 2018, washigtonpost.com. Accessed 21 Aug. 2018.

## CHAPTER 9. LOOKING TO THE FUTURE

1. Youkyung Lee. "Samsung Electronics Estimates 56 Percent Jump in Profit." *US News and World Report*, 6 Apr. 2018, usnews.com. Accessed 21 Aug. 2018.

2. Michael Moore. "What Is the IoT? Everything You Need to Know." *Tech Radar*, 9 Mar. 2018, techradar.com. Accessed 21 Aug. 2018.

3. Rachel Premack. "Why Samsung Thinks the Key to Its Future (and Profits) Could Be in the Auto Sector." *Forbes*, 7 Dec. 2017, forbes.com. Accessed 11 Apr. 2018.

4. Premack, "Why Samsung Thinks the Key to Its Future (and Profits) Could Be in the Auto Sector."

5. "Samsung SDI Unveils Innovative Battery Products at Detroit Motor Show." *Business Wire*, 14 Jan. 2018, businesswire.com. Accessed 11 Apr. 2018.

6. "More Than 3,000 Samsung Smart Schools Nurture the Talent of Tomorrow through Digital Education." *Samsung News*, 14 July 2017, news.samsung.com. Accessed 15 May 2018.

# INDEX

# ABOUT THE AUTHOR

## MICHAEL REGAN

Michael Regan worked as a community college and university career counselor before turning his attention to research and writing. He is especially interested in topics related to technology and current events. In his spare time, he enjoys watercolor painting, drawing, hiking, tai chi, and reading. He lives in southern Arizona with his spouse and two cats.